Healing Through Poetry

by

Deborah La'Sassier

PENMAN PUBLISHING, INC.

First Published 2001
Penman Publishing, Inc.
4159 Ringgold Road, Suite 104
Chattanooga, Tennessee 37412

Healing Through Poetry

by Deborah La'Sassier

ISBN: 0-9712808-2-7

Manufactured in the United States of America.

Printed by Penman Publishing, Inc.

Healing Through Poetry

Meaning to My Poetry

Before I tell you where I am going
Let me tell you where I've been.
Everything I am or ever hope to be
I owe it to you who had faith in me.
Not to mention the folks at work (19N)
Who let me write about their personal stuff.
You made my poetry come to life.
You shared your life and I began to write.
So here's to all my family and friends,
and special thanks go out to Nadine.
I can't forget Sue and her three sons,
Or Roz, about the man she loves.
I wrote about Sunitha's emotional pain.
And people learning how to swim above the rain.
I wrote about Alex being a Ghetto Princess.
And the price Tina paid, when her husband left her.
My mother's bad habit of trying not to smoke.
My husband's brain surgery, Gina and Robert going broke.
Eric growing up, Justina turning into a butterfly.
Michelle in Arizona, Paul and Bruce taking care of their mother.
These are just a few who made my poetry have meaning.
So once again I thank you for giving me my inspiration.

Gnashing My Teeth

My day is almost over, night has just begun.
I tried to write some thoughts down today
But inspiration just wouldn't come my way.
I wanted to write what was in my heart
Angry feelings were clogging up my thoughts.
I don't want to be angry, I hate being mad.
You just had to push me to my limits
You know my temper is very, very bad.
It's very hard for me to forget
And even harder for me to forgive.
You know what I always say
"Live and let die, not live and let live."
The next time you want to hurt my feelings
Just keep one thing in mind, I can be mad forever
And forever is a very long, long time.

Homosexuality

You left the kids and me for another man.
How can I get over this?
When I really don't fully understand?
It's a different kind of emotional pain.
I cry every time I think of you and that man.
When it first happened, I was angry with you
I was your wife for over seven years
Why didn't I see you weren't being for real?
We have two beautiful children,
How can I explain this to them?
That their father wants to be a she instead of a him?
I called you all kinds of horrid names
My feelings were hurt cause you left me for another man.
I didn't want you to confuse the kids
So I kept them away from you and your man.
I took it personal when you chose him over me
At the time I didn't understand about Homosexuality!

Young Dad

Dedicated to Mighty Mouse

I got married when I was only seventeen.
Not old enough to buy cigarettes
But old enough to be a married man.
My wife was only sixteen
Now she blames me for her lost hopes and dreams.
Today I turned twenty-one
I already have a daughter and three small sons.
Now I'm working two full-time jobs.
Having four kids is a lot of mental work
You don't see me laughing
This s### ain't no joke!
I know we got married way too young
We'll probably have problems
Until maturity sets in.
If I had it all to do over again, I wouldn't change a thing.
"You see, I love my wife and my four children!"

Lost Childhood

I'm tired of hearing you did the best you could
Look at me; I did the best I could too.
Now I'm grown with emotional scars
Trying to survive so my kids won't starve.
I tried not to raise them like you raised me.
I thought you were so mean,
I thought you hated me.
You made me grown before my time
I was mother and father to your tribe of nine.
I know you worked two jobs, day in and day out.
While I raised your kids, and cried my heart out.
By the time I was fifteen I was all burnt out.
I'm still trying to figure my childhood out!
Now I have problems and you wonder why?
I know you did the best you could
"But Mom, so did I."

Mama's Boy

When I was a little boy
My mom said never to follow the crowd.
She taught me to be my own person
And this stuck with me for a while.
I never had the chance to make mistakes
Mom always caught me before I fell.
I guess that was her way of teaching me
The difference between heaven and hell
Then I started following the wrong crowd
Getting into trouble and just acting wild.
One day I was in the wrong place at the wrong time.
You know the rest of the story,
I went Upstate and did some time.
Mama never said I told you so, I knew her heart was broken
Her eyes told me so. Ma came to visit every other week.
She made me strong when the system tried to make me weak.
I looked at my mom; she had tears in her eyes.
The next thing I knew we both began to cry.
I wiped away her tears, and held out my hands.
"Mama, please don't turn loose until I become a man!"

Mommy and my Mother

Dedicated to Marquia

Once there were two women, who never knew each other.
One you called Mommy,
The other you referred to as Mother.
The mother gave you life, a brilliant smile
Brown eyes and dimples, just like her.
The mommy taught you reality,
And there was "always a light at the end of the tunnel."
The mother gave you emotional scars,
The mommy calmed your fears.
The mommy saw your first tooth,
And watched you take your first step.
The mommy taught you never to lie
And to always walk with your head held high.
While the mother watched from afar
Through tear-stained eyes she whispered
"You are my shining star!"

My Best Friend

Dedicated to John M.

Last week I buried my best friend
Mom never came out of the coma
She stayed there until the very end.
God sent for her in her sleep one day.
I don't know, but I'm glad He planned it that way.
It was very hard seeing Mom like this
I silently asked God to make her first on His list.
This wasn't living—her breathing on a machine.
My sister wouldn't let go; she prayed for a miracle.
My mom's soul has gone on to a better place
I looked at her in her casket, and smiled.
She had peace written on her still face.
My mom will be the last thought of my day
When I wake in the morning
I'll thank God for giving her another day.
They say when you lose your mother
You have lost your best friend
I thank God my mother and I
Remained friends until the end.

Suicide Note

I saw tears in your eyes the other day
I asked, "Are you alright?"
You smiled and turned the other way
Then slowly walked out of my sight.
I had a feeling something was wrong.
At the time I didn't know what to say,
So I left you all alone.
You said you had a little pain in your heart
But eventually it would go away.
I offered you two Tylenols to ease the pain in some way.
Had I known, I would have told you,
"Tylenol doesn't ease emotional pain."
You said you needed some time to think
You asked me to give you some space.
I didn't want to leave you,
Cause you had a peculiar look on your face.
You said you felt a little better,
And for me not to worry so much.
The next day you left a suicide note,
Said you couldn't take it anymore.
You loaded your gun, pointed it to your head
And gently closed your bedroom door...

Sunitha

Look at you standing there with your arrogant self
Breaking porcelain dolls, and putting them on the shelf.
If I told you how much I loved you,
Would you still be in love with me?
Or if I broke your heart tomorrow,
Would you finally set my soul free?
Love don't love nobody,
Trust me I didn't make up the rules.
I loved and lost the hard way.
Loving you slowly turned my brown eyes blue.
I don't regret falling in love with you;
As a matter of fact, you made many of my dreams come true.
There you were standing six foot two
Looking so dark and so fine.
The moment our eyes met, I knew in my heart
One day I would make you all mine.
Nothing lasts forever, and tomorrow never comes.
I loved and lost the hard way
Now it's time for me to move on...

The Rainbow

I was raised with two mommies
That was the norm for me
My life was very happy, for a little kid of three.
When I started school, the kids use to tease me.
My mom was called a lesbian
So the little kids wouldn't play with me.
At the time I didn't know what it meant.
The way the kids would say it
I thought my mommy was a lizard or a snake.
My two moms sat me down to have a long talk.
They explained their lifestyle to me
In a way I could figure it out.
Being a lesbian just means she would rather
Be with another woman than another man.
I didn't grow up with any hang-ups.
Now I'm married with two kids of my own.
My kids are very lucky
They have three grandmas!

Unrequited Love

Dedicated to Sonny

We broke up again for the very last time
I'm tired of being hurt; I'm tired of your lies.
I tried to forget you, every way I could.
I even tried dating again, just to get me out of this mood.
But every man I dated, he reminded me of you.
Needless to say, no one will ever fill your shoes.
I know one day I'll get over you, and I'll learn to love again.
But while all this is taking place, please
Don't ask me to be your friend.
Cause a friend wouldn't do what you did to me
Instead of being punished, you walked away Scot free.
God only knows what was going through my head.
The night I came by and found that woman in your bed.
I was so hurt I just wanted to die
But all I could do wass hang my head down and cry.

Phobias

"You have nothing to fear but fear itself."
I read somewhere in a book.
Yet my fears are very real to me
I'm doing my very best to cope.
My anxiety is sometimes irrational
Sometimes the situation carries no danger to me at all.
Still I'm afraid of so many things,
Like snakes, elevators and small dogs.
To you these things may seem trivial
But my fears are very real.
I'm afraid of public transportation
So I walk wherever I have to go.
I stay in the house all day
Even though I'm afraid to be alone.
I'm a telephone operator
Even though I fear talking on the phone.
Some fears I try to overcome
How else will I earn my income?
I'm afraid of small dogs so I have a cat.
I'm afraid of spiders—they give me anxiety attacks.
I know these fears are just in my head
Maybe one day, I won't be so afraid.

Tee

Dedicated to my Grandson

Let me tell you about my favorite little guy.
He talks all the time, and that ain't no lie.
When he was a baby he never went to sleep.
I would rock him in my arms until I felt asleep.
When his mommy took away his bottle
Granddaddy went and bought him another.
Him and Keya grew up like sister and brother.
My little guy has a brother he loves very much.
He lives with his grandmother in Coram, New York
My little guy and his brother went away to camp
They had lots of fun and they just got back.
Tee learned to water ski, he slept in a cabin
He roasted hot dogs and he shot a bow and arrow.
He went on a boat, and had lots of fun.
He played basketball, one on one.
I heard him ask his mommy,
"Now what am I going to do for fun?"

Thanks Mom

Everything I am or ever hope to be
I owe it all to my mother,
She did a hell of a job raising me.
I will never forget the look on Dad's face
When he asked me to choose between his or her place.
I looked at Dad, and then I looked at her.
It wasn't a choice; I went to live with Mother.
Dad had left many times before
I knew Mom would never walk out that door.
Mom raised us the best she could.
The sacrifices she made, I could never repay her.
She worked two jobs to put us through college.
She never mentioned Dad, and she never remarried.
We all went to college—that was my mother's dream.
Next Thursday my Mom will turn ninety-three.
The system wanted to put Mom in a nursing home.
"Are you crazy," I said. My mother has three sons.
There's no way you'll put my mom is a home.

Looking Over My Shoulder

I left for work as I do every morning.
I felt someone staring, so I looked over my shoulder
I turned around to see who it was
It was the brother across the street
I think his name was Troy.
This went on for many months
He never said a word; he just stood there and watched.
After awhile I didn't see Troy anymore.
Several weeks later I was walking my dog.
I saw him staring from the side of his car.
Again I looked over my shoulder
To let the brother know I noticed.
With a silent smile on his face, Troy introduced himself.
He said he was shy, and I scared him away.
He stole glances at me each and every day.
Troy said I was pretty, but I looked mean and tough.
He didn't have the courage to ask me out.
Each time I looked over my shoulder at Troy,
I thought to myself,
"Well, come on and say something, boy!"

He Said She Said

Sometimes we see things that aren't really there.
Or repeat something said we know was not fair.
We make accusations
By thoughts planted in our heads.
We believe these thoughts
To be what was really said.
When we hear someone lie
With a smile on her face
We believe it to be true,
Not questioning the rest.
Do I believe what I thought I saw?
Should I believe what you thought you heard?
That lie spread like wildfire that week.
She said you said her husband was cheating.
Now they are in court dividing up the children.
In the future I'll just sit back and wait.
If anyone wants me to know something
I'll hear it from them straight!

A Lie is a Lie

I would rather have a shabby truth than a dressed up lie.
They say the truth hurts that why most people lie.
But in the long run, what about that lie?

>Personally speaking, I try not to lie
>   A friend lied to me once and betrayed my trust
>Now don't get me wrong, I've told my share of lies
>   But between you and me, a lie is a lie

I saw my old man on Main Street the other day.
He was smiling and grinning in some woman's face.
When he finally got home I asked where had he been.
He said in Patchogue shooting pool with a friend.
I called him a liar and demanded he tell me the truth.
"I swear I was in Patchogue playing pool with Bruce!"
I looked at him and smiled to myself,
"You just got busted, I saw you myself!"
"I'm sorry I lied, but I was afraid to tell you the truth
I didn't mean to hurt you, Baby; I swear that's the truth."

>Personally speaking, I try not to lie
>   A friend lied to me once and betrayed my trust
>Now don't get me wrong, I've told my share of lies
>   But between you and me, a lie is a lie

A One-Woman Man

There was this young woman
Who tried to break my style.
She thought she could tame me
Cause my lifestyle was outrageously wild.
She tried to make me into something I wasn't
I told her the worst thing she could do
"Was to tame this here brother!"
I told her I couldn't stay in one place too long.
She said give her a chance; she would change my mind.
She told me she loved me three weeks after we met.
This woman was going too fast
I needed more time to contemplate.
I tried to be totally honest with her.
She asked me if I loved her,
I told her I wasn't sure.
She said, "Move in and we'll just be friends."
By the end of the week I was ready to leave again.
I'm not a one-woman man,
I tried to tell you from the start.
Don't try to change me,
And I won't try to break your heart.

A World Without

Have you ever thought how frightening it would be
Living in a world without friends or enemies?
People who are incapable of feeling
Spend most of their lives being miserable and unhappy.
There is no sorrow or regrets
When emotions are hidden and you lose self-respect.
People could not be diverted or entertained
When there is a thin line between the sane and the insane.
A world without fear
Would be a horrible place to live.
People would do whatever they want,
People would do whatever they feel.
A world without ethics would be a debauched place to live
In a world like this only corruption would live.
No merit, no conscience, no emotional feelings.
In a world without, there's no happy ending.

All Grown Up

Dedicated to my son Eric

You went from a messy little kid
To graduating from the Marines.
Plenty of things happened in the middle,
I'll keep it between you and me.
You had so much energy;
You made everything around you shine.
You had more friends than the law allowed.
There was always a smile on your face,
You were always there to brighten up someone's day.
Have I told you lately how proud I am?
You've grown into a man of quality and ambition.
When you were younger, I had my doubts.
You were always into something;
I couldn't quite figure you out.
After Holy Angels Bellport didn't have a chance.
You burst through the doors and hardly ever went to class.
You broke little girls' hearts like they were a dime a dozen.
By the time you were seventeen,
You had dated two dozen.
You started things and would always quit.
I was afraid your dreams would end up like that.
You proved me wrong, you decided to grow up.
Now you're with MTV, making all the bucks!

Arizona

Dedicated to Michelle

You were my whole world—I loved you all my life.
After basic training you asked me to be your wife.
We moved to Arizona, it was a long way from home.
I missed my family; I started to feel all alone.
Then came our baby, now this house was a home.
I gave all my attention to the baby, leaving you all alone.
After I gave to the baby, there was nothing left for you.
We moved back home, now the baby was my life.
I stopped being your friend; I stopped being your wife.
We began to argue, then fuss and fight.
I left with the baby; I didn't want this kind of life.
We did things we could never forgive each other for.
Though we still loved each other,
We just couldn't make it anymore.
Our paths will never cross again, we will never be lovers.
But we'll always be good friends.

All Seven of Them

I work three jobs to support my seven kids.
Yea, I sleep to noon on the weekends,
Cause my body needs the rest.
I'm here all weekend with literally no life.
Yea, my husband ran off with Tyrone's wife.
He left me here with these seven kids.
No money, no note, not even a reason.
Sometimes the kids drive me crazy,
They make me want to pack up and leave.
Still I love my children, all seven of them.
Yea, they have different daddies,
But it's none of your concern.
I'm raising them alone, all seven of them.
I work three jobs; I don't have a life.
I've never played the part of the abandoned wife.
We never have enough of anything,
It seems we always need.
But we do have each other, and our home is full of love.
I love my kids with all my heart
Yea, all seven of them.

Bad Mood Swings

When I enter my front door
I feel my moods starting to change.
I don't know what is happening to me.
My moods are so very strange.
My little girl runs up to me,
"Mommy, how was your day, did you miss me?"
With a frown on my face,
And my moods really swinging
I yell at my daughter and hurt her feelings.
When my husband comes home
She runs up to him,
Daddy, "Mommy's in a bad mood,
I don't know what I did!"
"Don't worry, baby, it's nothing you did;
Mommy gets in those moods every now and then."
In her little voice she said to him,
"That doesn't make it right to hurt my feelings,
Or make her little girl feel bad.
Daddy, when I grow up,
I don't want to get what Mommy has!"

Baseball on a Cloudy Day

I can't make things right, if you keep making them wrong.
I thought we made peace, why let this linger on?
I said I was sorry for making you feel bad,
But you hurt me too, and I was willing to let it pass.
Two wrongs don't make a right
Be careful what you say, cause you can't take words back.
Whatever it takes for us to get over this,
Let's not waste another day,
This doesn't make any sense for us to go on this way.
We both said things that really cut deep
You can play on words or learn to forgive and forget.
It's really up to you, cause I've made my peace.

Basic Human Rights

My mama was raped,
Her husband and son were sold away.
Master's blood ran through my veins
So my mama and me were allowed to stay.
Mama worked in Master's house all day and all night.
When I turned four years old,
Master taught me to read and write.
Though I was Master's child
I wasn't treated with any special rights,
Most of the time I was hidden out of sight.
My mama called me her blue-eyed baby girl.
She said I was all she had left in this world.
Master sold her husband right after I was born.
She said she would never love again,
Cause her heart was severely torn.
Master was never a father, but he treated me all right.
When he looked into my eyes,
He saw his own blue eyes staring back.
I was too black to be white and too white to be black
And because of this, I was denied my basic rights.

To Be or Not to Be

Instead of peaking from that closet,
Why don't you come on out.
True friends won't judge you,
And anyone else shouldn't even count.
You worry about what society says.
Do they put food on your table?
Or checks in your mail?
Why worry about things you have no control.
When you give a person that much power
Eventually they'll take over your soul.
There are certain things you can never change
Your sex preference is one of them.
Don't let people make you feel ashamed.
Accept who you are and get on with your life.
Who said you have to have a husband?
It's your choice if you want a wife.
Don't let people interfere in your life
Unless they're paying your rent,
They really don't have the right.
True friends won't judge what you have or haven't done.
Don't be afraid to love who you want.
Life is too short to worry about unnecessary stuff.

Beauty's Only Skin Deep

Who sets the standards to what's pretty or not?
Is a pretty face all society can see?
Or is it what's inside that makes her pretty?
We judge people by their personal appearance.
That doesn't say much about our society, now does it?
What about the heavyset girl with the pretty face?
Society rejects her cause she doesn't have a small waist.
How about the Spanish girl with the long wavy hair.
Is she judged by her beauty or just her long hair?
What about the pretty Haitian girl with the strong accent?
Are you judging her because of her speech and dialect?
What about the pretty Jewish girl with the curly hair?
So her nose is not like yours, why worry who cares!
And what about the pretty girl with the ebony skin?
Society thinks she is not pretty.
Cause she doesn't have blond hair and fair skin.
I saw a pretty woman just the other day
But when she opened her mouth, her beauty escaped.
What's the point of having a pretty face
When you are missing character, morals and good taste?

Betrayal

We have shared a long history together
We have been each other's rock.
When you were in the hospital,
I was there around the clock.
When you were in your time of need
I promised to be there and to never leave.
We shared many times as true friends do.
My man was off limits, I thought that you knew.
You couldn't stay away from him
You wore halter-tops and tight designer jeans.
You did everything to get his attention.
He came back and told me of all your intentions.
After all we've been through
Your true colors finally came out.
I saw the real you, and what you were all about.
I treated you like family; you were a sister I never had.
You made the mistake of betraying me
Now our friendship is a thing of the past.

Between You and Me

Please don't get mad
When I do or say the wrong thing.
Sometimes I speak before I think,
Then I hurt your feelings.
Life has a way of working itself out
I did a good job,
You and your brother turned out all right.
Just between you and me
I'm proud of the way you turned out to be.
You've raised your children very well
They've stayed out of trouble,
They've stayed out of jail.
I hope God gives us many more days.
I'd like to get to know about you and your ways.
All in all, I'll say it again
I'm sorry for the past,
And thank God we are now friends.

Big Girls Don't Cry

As a little girl I climbed tall trees,
Wore faded blue jeans with holes in the knees.
I wore my hair tied back, covered with a Mets baseball cap.
I never wore a dress except on Sundays, or
Maybe during the week if company was coming.
I played baseball instead of with Barbie.
I always hung out with the boys,
I never had time to write in a dairy.
My dad taught me not ever to cry.
Whatever happens, "Never show your weaker side."
As an adult I found it very difficult to cry.
Any emotions I had, I kept them inside.
I was sensitively hurt once, and I wanted to cry.
Something painful happened between me and my guy.
Before the first tear fell, I heard my father's voice saying:
"Big girls don't cry," and this stuck with me forever.
So now I'm a big girl with no emotions at all.
If and when I do cry, I cry behind closed doors.

Big Ma

Grandma raised me since I was two years old.
She was the only mother I've ever really known.
My mommy was on drugs, she used to smoke the pipe.
Grandma didn't want me raised
In an environment like that.
Grandma taught me the basics in life.
She didn't want me growing up wasting my life.
Grandma said Mom loved me with all her heart;
She just couldn't choose between me and her drugs.
I didn't see Mom again until I was almost four.
She was on Forty-second Street with a customer.
When I turned eighteen, I went looking for my mom.
I wanted to get rid of this anger
That was buried inside for so long.
I never found my mother. I heard she died three months before.
When I left for college Grandma gave me this note.
It was the answer to why my mother gave me up.
It wasn't because she didn't love me
Truth is, she loved me too much!

Black Dialect

I heard a conversation
Between two brothers today.
Though they spoke English,
It didn't sound the same.
I didn't understand everything they said.
I'm sure it was English with a lot of broken verbs.
The conversation sounded like poetry in motion.
I saw them give hugs like it was some sort of ritual.
They were shaking hands to an unheard beat.
I tried not to judge as I listened to them speak.
This language was different, exciting and diverse.
They took the fewest words possible
Making them mean the most.
Black dialect is commonly used today.
Who's to say what's wrong or right?
We possess the technique of bringing this language to life.

Blue-Eyed Soul Sistah

They called her my blue-eyed soul sister
I never understood why.
We both saw life through the same color eyes.
She could double Dutch, and would corn braid my hair.
We had slumber parties all of the time.
I slept at her house, she slept at mine.
We enjoyed playing together each and every day.
There was never the mention of color,
Till a stranger brought it up one day.
As years went on, we grew up together,
When you saw one, you always saw the other.
During high school we shared an even closer bond.
Then after graduation we both left home.
We remained friends for a very long time.
She was godmother to my daughter
I was godmother to her son.
They still call her my blue-eyed soul sistah
But between you and me,
I just call her my friend Ruthie.

Brain Surgery

Dedicated to my husband Michael

I may forget what you told me today.
I just had brain surgery, so give me a break.
I know I asked you that question before.
But give me a break; some of my memory is gone.
What did you say happened yesterday?
Do I take the same medicine I took yesterday?
Sorry, baby, I forgot to turn off the stove.
And why can't I go out to scythe my lawn?
You've asked that same question five times already.
I'm fine, baby, but you're driving me crazy.
I'll be back to myself; you just wait and see.
Just leave me alone, you're bothering me.
I'm sorry, baby, I just want you to be all right.
The surgery you had gave me an awful fright.
"Baby, why don't you tell me what you want me to do?"
I just had brain surgery, and I'm still a little confused.

Bud...Wise...Zer

I can't believe after all we've been through
You would rather sit by that pond
And drink a beer or two.
You don't share your problems or your pain.
You hide behind that can of beer,
Just wasting your life away.
Sometimes I look out the kitchen window
And see you sitting by the pond,
And really wish that we could talk.
But you would rather I left you alone.
You hide your emotions very well,
But your eyes tell me you're going through hell.
So there you sit by the pond,
Drinking your beer, and talking to your frogs.
Pretty soon the boys will be gone,
I'll be here all alone
You'll be down there by the pond.
Drinking your beer and talking to the frogs.

Choices I Made

My mom said as a child, I was always alone.
I never played with other kids
Only the ones who were make believe.
When I became older I asked my mom,
"Didn't you think it was strange, me always being alone?"
Mom said I was very shy, Dad said I was mean as hell.
Mom said, "That was strange for a little girl!"
I had a quick temper and chased everyone away.
I gave the impression that I really didn't care.
When I got older I decided to change,
I controlled my temper and started making friends.
Then I saw what people were all about.
They had too much drama, plus they lied a lot.
So I choose to be alone most of the time.
I can relax with my thoughts,
And leave all that drama alone.

Conclusion

We have come to the end of our conclusion...
I can't change you; believe me I've tried.
I can't live this life style;
It's driving me wild.
We've been separated for almost three years.
My feelings are gone,
My heart is now empty.
We met at a time I really needed a friend.
My home life was miserable
I needed a new beginning.
Thanks to you I went back to school,
Got my diploma and started to feel good.
Please don't get me wrong
I appreciate everything you're done.
But I've outgrown you;
It's time for me to move on.

The Conversation

"I don't know what this world is coming to,
Babies having babies."
"Lard, ain't that the truth."
"I saw this little boy selling drugs on the street.
The saddest thing about it,
He was only five, maybe six."
"I read in the papers the other day,
This little kid killed his mother
Cause she wouldn't let him go outside to play."
"Lard, you don't say!"
"And what about the kids taking guns to school
Stealing other kids' sneakers,
Just acting a fool.
Just the other day this kid broke into my house,
Stole my stuff, and threatened my life."
"Lard, you don't say!"
"Who can we blame for the outcome of these kids?"
They only know what they believe to be real.
Daddy's gone, taking care of someone else's kids.
Mama's working three jobs trying to make ends meet.
Grandma don't have time, she's trying to live large."
So who can we blame, who's at fault?

Cookie Monster

Dedicated to Julie and her mother

The worst thing in my life I've ever had to do,
Was put you in a nursing home;
I could no longer take care of you.
I look into your eyes and I'm afraid to see
One day you may remember or recognize me.
The tables have turned, now I'm taking care of you.
It's no big deal; that's what families do.
I got married the other day,
And couldn't share my happiness with you.
The day I came to tell you,
You didn't remember my name or who I was to you.
I know there will be days, you won't know me
Or what I have or haven't done.
I thank God for our past memories
Cause I'll have them when everything is said and done.
Sometimes when I come to visit with you,
You have a faraway look in your eyes.
I sense you don't remember me; I just smile and cry inside.
There is nothing I wouldn't do for you
You are my cookie monster, and I'll always love you.

Is This a Female Thang?

Dedicated to Mike

I'm really getting tired of all these attitudes.
Everybody's angry and always in a bad mood.
This stuff ain't cool; I never know what to say.
You three women make me want to run away!
I have to be careful of everything I say.
The wrong word or expression makes emotions go astray.
Keya gets mad and starts slamming the pots and pans.
Then Kim walks around yelling and screaming.
And you start crying, making everyone feel bad.
"Give me a break, I'm only the Dad!"
You three women with these attitudes
Yesterday alone I counted three or four.
I really don't know what to say or do,
"Is this a female thang?" I keep asking you.
And then (snap), like that, everything is cool.
You three are laughing and in a good mood.
Believe me, I just don't understand.
Then again, "Is this a female thang?"

Call Me Sometime

Dedicated to my mother Lera

Don't send me flowers
When I'm dead and gone.
Call me once in awhile
When you know I'm all alone.
Call me sometime
In case I'm sick with the flu.
Don't just think of me on Mother's Day,
I'm getting older now,
I'm not promised many more days.
I'd like to see my grandkids once in awhile.
Otherwise I may not recognize them
If and when they decide to call.
Invite me over for dinner on Sundays,
I can sit in the backyard
And watch the grandkids play and run.
If nothing else, just call me to say, "Hi,
Do you need something, Mother?"
And then say goodbye.

Death and Dying

Tell me,
Tell you what?
How does it feel?
"How does what feel?"
How does it feel to die?
So many things have died
Why should you be concerned?
Then tell me what things have died?
Emotions die,
Dreams die,
Flowers die, Chatty Cathy died.
Spirits die,
Friendships die,
Old typewriters die, my second grade teacher died.
Goldfish die,
Old records die,
Fake eyelashes die, my 1969 Mustang died.
Grandmother's die,
Girls in tight jeans die, Christ died.
So many things have died, why should you be concerned?

Death Came Stealing

I prayed to leave this body everyday.
Then death came stealing late one night.
I guess my prayers were answered that night.
I knew in my heart everything was going to be fine.
My only regret was leaving my family behind.
Death kept knocking, over and over again
My husband refused to let death in.
My husband said, "Please, I can't let you go.
My heart will be empty my life will be no more."
I motioned for my husband to come closer to me.
I put his hand on my chest to feel my final heartbeat.
"I won't let you go," he cried out to me.
I prayed to God to keep you with me.
I want to go with death; it will be better for me.
Please, don't make me suffer more than need be.
My husband looked into my eyes, and all he saw was pain.
An empty shell of what used to be me
Then he decided to let death in.

Different Way of Life

When I was married, life used to be so easy
For me and my four kids.
After the divorce, my opulent lifestyle ceased.
I went from a six-bedroom house,
With two cars, and a jeep
To a two bedroom apartment
Living from paycheck to paycheck.
I work everyday to support my four kids.
I don't get much alimony or child support.
I can't get what I need,
And my kids can't get what they want.
Being impoverished has changed my outlook on life.
It's a different way of living; it's a lot of sacrifice.
Between you and me, I don't want to get used to this way of life.
Yes, I do appreciate life more now than I did before.
But I wish I didn't have
To experience it being poor.

Divorce

I don't blame you for the divorce
I had a drinking problem that nearly destroyed us.
Now that it's over, and I think about the past,
Your life must have been hell.
How did you survive?
For ten long years we stuck it out
You were there with me, when my family ran out.
We stayed together; we did what we had to do.
I only regret the time we wasted.
You blaming me, me blaming you.
Then my drinking got way out of control.
I lost everything I had,
Then I began to lose my inner soul.
The best thing in my life you did for me.
You let me hit rock bottom, to see if I could swim.
Not only did I waste my life
But your life was put on hold.
So thank you for divorcing me,
You actually saved my soul.

Long Distance Love

Dedicated to Sal

It's a long ride to Queens,
I'll see you next week.
I'm not feeling the traffic,
I'm tired and I want to sleep.
You have to work midnight shift again?
Oh well, I'll see you some time next week.
The next thing I knew, three months had gone by.
It was my fault, I had too many alibis.
I guess I made it easy for that woman to come by.
You said I left you high and dry.
So you didn't see me for a couple of months.
I thought our relationship was based on trust.
You'll never know the extent of my pain.
It was an awful feeling, my heart wouldn't stop aching.
I don't want to ever experience again!
So listen carefully, my sweetheart from Queens,
I'm only going to say this once, so please try to listen.
"Yea, word up!"
"I'll forgive you this time, for betraying my trust."

Wake Up and Stop Tripping

Does it really matter how much we go to church
Or how often we sit and pray
Or whether or not we help our neighbor
Who said we would be judged that way?
Suppose there were no future or past.
We just lived for present moment,
Just waiting for time to pass.
Suppose there was no day or night,
Suppose there was no wrong or right.
We live, we die; we laugh, we cry.
We try to reach for that pie in the sky.
"Yo, wake up and stop tripping!"
No one said life was going to be easy.
Sometimes you have to take the bitter with the sweet.
You play the cards life has dealt to you,
And if you can't win,
You can always try to cheat!

Does Your Man

Dedicated to Alex and Erick

I'm getting tired of this drama
It's time he knows how I feel.
If he can't treat me as an equal
Perhaps I should pack up and leave.
"Do you love him?" Debbie asked me one day.
Does he treat your son well?
And act like a daddy.
Does he make you laugh on rainy days?
Does he listen to you bitch when you've had a bad day?
Does he cook dinner when you are working late?
So what if it's Stove Top, at least it's a plate.
Does he tell you he loves you at least once a week?
Has he ever asked your mother to come out to stay?
If you can agree with some of the things I said.
Consider yourself lucky,
And stop some of that bitching!

Dressed up Lie

I looked to you for all the right answers
All I got was the shabby truth and dressed up lies.
"Look me straight in my face," I demanded.
And still you told me lies.
All I ever wanted was the truth, all I got was whys.
I tried to see the truth in you, but all I got were lies.
You promised to love me forever, in fact
"Till death do us part." Instead of loving me forever
You constantly broke my heart.
Whenever we went out to a party,
You were always in some other man's garden.
You picked fresh flowers every chance you got.
And threw me out, like old bath water.
I just turned my back for a minute
You were grinning and taking down phone numbers
Like you won some lotto ticket.
Love helps you to forgive and forget.
I don't know baby,
"But I'm getting tired of this sh##!"

Emotional Colors

Colors represent my emotional moods
So each day I dress according to this rule.
Mondays, I want to feel enthusiasm and zeal
Red is the color and that's how I feel.
Tuesday, after an exhausting day at work
I like to feel nice and mellow
I find intensity in the color yellow.
Wednesday, I need a little boost of energy
Saffron is the color and I wear it with ease.
It's virtuous energy and it calms down my fears.
Thursdays, I always wear the color green,
It represents control and manipulation.
Fridays, I like to wear the color blue.
It ends all boundaries and denotes patience too.
Saturdays, I'm always in a no nonsense mood.
I wear basic black from head to toe;
It puts me in the mood of extensive control.
On the Lord's Day, I always wear white.
White puts me in a mood of divinity.
After a week of drama,
I like to feel some spiritual healing.

Pain is Pain

Regardless of what you do or say,
Emotional and physical pain is the same.
Physical pain will only last a minute,
While emotional pain will destroy your spirits.
You said some insensitive things last night.
You hurt my feelings; I cried most of the night.
I've asked you many times before,
Think before you cut me down with words!
Each time you hurt me emotionally with words,
It takes a little from my heart, it makes me not love.
If you continue to do this
There will be nothing left inside of me.
Regardless of what you do or say,
"Pain is pain!"
I can't express it any other way.

End of the Road

Whatever decision I have to make
Someone will be hurt,
There's no compensating.
I have to leave;
I have to get myself together.
Who are we fooling?
This marriage is over.
The decision I make will have an impact on us all.
I've tried to find solutions
It's like running into a brick wall.
I've thought of my options,
I've weighed everything out.
Sure, I could keep you happy
But, doesn't my happiness count?
We've both made mistakes
We can never take back.
I can try to forgive you,
But it's a long road back.
But either way, some changes have to be made.
I can't continue to live like this,
You have to at least meet me half way.

Excess Baggage

I have to get rid of some baggage today.
I'll clean up my house,
Starting first with the attic.
Emotions have been buried since early childhood.
I have to let go of these memories;
I'm ready to feel good!
I've buried things in my subconscious mind,
These memories prevent me from feeling inside.
My life will never be whole and complete
Until I let go of this emotional pain and self defeat.
I've built up walls I have to learn to tear down.
It will take awhile; it's been buried for a very long time.
I took everything down from the attic today.
I guess tomorrow I'll start to clean out my basement.

Face of Time

At night she wears a face of stone
Not allowing anyone to enter.
She rather be left alone.
She looks in the mirror and thinks of the time
When she was young and beautiful
When she had time on her side.
Always full of hopes and dreams
She knew where she was going
Cause she knew where she had been.
She looked in the mirror and saw a different face
She began to weep and sob,
"What happened to my face?"
Sixty years had somehow gone by,
She thought to herself as she began to cry.
She doesn't want to grow old,
She doesn't want to lose her young face.
Without a beginning there could be no end
We have to grow old so a new life can begin.

Reawakening

Dedicated to my son Eric, thank you

I'm most irate when I pretend to be at ease.
My heart aches more when I try to please.
The audience keeps laughing; that's well and fine.
But it's drama not comedy and I'm falling behind.
They say ignorance is bliss
And a wise woman's cheeks are never dry.
Well, I've seen the good and evil of love
Now I wish I had closed my eyes.
A woman demands attention,
And all the love she can bear.
No man or woman to be equal,
So she alone and reap his care.
But once the ransom had been paid
Unlike selfish love, more demands were made.
I stagger from the love of my man, demanding my attention.
Yes, his desires were grand,
But the nails were from my foundation.
You can't build a relationship
On mistrust and broken promises.
After a lifetime of living in misery,
You soon run out of options.

Trying to Grow Up

You were higgledy-piggledy like your brother Eric.
I never knew girls kept their room so messy.
At three years old you were singing and dancing.
You smiled and pointed to your dimples
Whenever you were around strangers.
You made everything around you shine.
You had charisma and style.
You never gave up, you never allowed yourself to fall.
You were never a quitter, and you always stood tall.
Though you had a bad habit of believing in people.
"Everybody that smiles in your face is not your friend."
I told you this over and over again!
I know sometimes you may think I'm wrong.
Just take my advice until you turn twenty-one.

First Love

Dedicated to my childhood sweetheart

His name was Sylvester
He lived across town.
A good-looking feller
Light skin and brown eyes.
All the girls chased after him
But I was the one
Who got his full attention.
Sylvester walked me home from school one day.
My father got upset,
When he saw us talking in the driveway.
Dad said I couldn't see Sylvester anymore,
I was too young to have a boyfriend
So Dad's answer was no.
I continued to see him everyday after school.
There was something about him
That made our friendship feel real.
We remained friends till the end of the school year.
Before school started again, we moved away from there
It took awhile to get over him,
I couldn't stop crying, I couldn't stop the tears.
It's ten years later and when I think about Sylvester
It's a shame I moved away,
Cause I would have married him one day

First Real Fight

My first real fight was with a boy name Luther.
We fought on the playground
A block from the schoolyard.
I don't remember what the fight was about.
Luther said he liked me, so I started the fight.
By the end of junior high, we had become friends.
During my senior year,
Luther asked me to his prom.
"But please," he said,
"Leave your boxing gloves at home!"
We laughed and talked about our first fight.
The day I tripped him as he was getting off his bike,
I threw the baseball and hit him on his leg,
And when I threw the bat, I almost hit him in his head.
We went to McDonalds one day for lunch.
Luther brought me French fries and a large cherry coke.
The next day I told my brother to beat Luther up.
All these things I did to him,
And all Luther wanted was to be my boyfriend.

Fly High

Dedicated to my friend Dora

As parents we teach our children to fly high.
To set their goals and reach for the sky.
When that day finally comes
We're not prepared for the empty nest syndrome.
When you told me you were joining the air force,
I was happy and sad all at once.
When that day finally came,
I wasn't prepared for my empty feelings.
There is a special bond between a mother and her son.
It cannot be defined or ever misunderstood.
I never knew it would hurt this bad.
My heart feels empty; I'm lonely and sad.
I miss you more than I could ever say.
You moved all the way to Texas.
That's a long way from the nest!

Forty Nine...Fifty

At first I was dreading my birthday.
I can't believe I'm turning fifty!
I thought to myself,
It's really not that bad.
I'm happy with my life,
I'm even happy with my past.
My dreams for my kids have all come true.
They are settled in their lives
Doing what they should do.
Michael is great, I guess you can say.
He's been my soul mate from the very first day.
We've been together for over twenty-two years.
He's been my friend;
He's always kept it real!
If I had my life to do all over again.
I wouldn't change a thing.
My life has been very happy.
Yes, today is my birthday, but guess what?
"I look good at fifty!"

Friday Night

Dedicated to Key

It's Friday night and I'm here alone.
Sitting in my room,
Hoping the telephone would ring.
Too young to date, too old for cartoons.
I feel I'm in the middle of a big typhoon.
It's Friday night and I'm all alone.
Daddy's watching basketball on TV
Mommy's working on her poetry.
She's in a whole different world.
I have to make an appointment to even talk to her.
Terrance and Brandon aren't here this week.
There's no one here to pick a fight with or tease.
Kim just left; I think she went to Queens.
There's nothing to do but sit in this room.
Ring...Ring. I hope its Hakaam,
He makes me laugh whenever I talk to him.
He's home alone too, on this Friday night!
Is that what being a teenager is about!

Get Over It

Whenever we're together, you bring up the past.
Stuff that happened twenty years ago,
Why can't you let it past?
Why bring this stuff up, there's nothing I can do.
So your daddy left you, he ran out on me too.
I'm sorry for the pain he caused, what more can I do.
I did the best with what I had,
You're not the only one that had it bad.
I worked two jobs day in and day out.
I took care of you when your daddy ran off.
I never had a life, and I never complained.
So get over the drama, get over your pain.
Just between you and me, here's a little of my history.
I too was raised without a dad,
Three sisters in one bed.
And you think you have it bad?
So whatever you thought you missed out on in life.
Get over the pain and start enjoying your life.

Ghetto Princess

Dedicated to my daughter Alex

I had two choices very early in life.
I either learned how to cry, or learn how to fight.
At twelve I was the oldest of sixteen grandkids.
Aunts and uncles grew up in the same bed.
Yea, I'm a little rough around the edges
When you're raised in the Ghetto,
You have to always be ready.
Yea, I'm loud and I say what's on my mind.
I don't like to bull s... so don't waste my time.
My life has always been a struggle
I had uncles and cousins raised without morals.
So if I seem a little Ghetto, please understand why.
Life was always a fight to the finish,
And only the strong survived.
My dad Mike left a long time ago,
My mom Diane raised me alone, you know.
My mom had her own problems, I don't judge her anymore.
She was the oldest of eighteen kids, need I say any more?
Yea, I'm a Ghetto Princess, but I'm one no more!

Going Home

After many years of suffering with pain
I grew tired of living; I grew tired of this pain.
I prayed to God each and every night
To take away this cancer, to make me all right.
This cancer was slowing killing me
My body hurt.
My mind and my thoughts were now empty.
I constantly asked God to take me away
I couldn't live like this, there had to be a better way.
My prayers weren't answered, God must have looked away.
Did he think he was doing me a favor,
Giving me one more suffering day?
I'm tired of all this misery; I'm tired of all this pain.
I can't eat, I can't sleep; this cancer is driving me insane.
I had chemo just last week.
I'm losing my hair, and I still can't eat.
I've lost sixty-three pounds; I'm down to size two.
God, please let me go, I'm begging you.

Gossip

Don't you just hate it when you walk into a room?
People turn and stare cause they were talking about you.
Don't you just hate people who love to tell lies?
Why can't they mind their own business,
And quit worrying about mine?
I don't know why they don't just get a life.
Instead they're all up in my business,
Worrying about what I did the other night.
If these people have so much free time on their hands,
Why don't they get a hobby, or find them a man.
Cause the way it stands now
They're up in everybody's business.
One day the right person will be talked about
And there will be severe consequences!

Greener Grass

I look in the mirror every morning
And before I start my day,
I promise to do something nice for me,
Cause I'm the only one who can make my day.
I tell myself, and I truly believe
We control our own destiny.
How we think and how we want to feel,
It's up to us to repudiate negative energy.
You don't have the power to determine how I feel
I decide what I'm not going to feel.
I try to be positive throughout my whole day.
I stay away from negative feedback
Sometimes it brings out the worst in me.
I don't try to keep up with the Jones's
I heard they have problems of their own.
Sometimes what we are looking for
Is really right here at home.
If the grass looks greener on the other side
Just water your lawn a little more!

Hands on the Clock

I woke up this morning; and couldn't get out of bed.
My baby was crying, cause she wanted to be fed.
The dog kept barking, and wouldn't stop.
It was twelve o'clock and I couldn't get up.
In the past three weeks, I've felt extremely elated.
I've had episodes of mood swings, and no appetite lately.
My reduced motivations were driving me crazy.
My depressed moods feel like utter despair.
The simple things I can no longer do.
Cook, clean the house,
Take care of the kids are just a few.
I felt loneliness and boredom
I felt worthless and afraid.
I spent most of the day sleeping;
I couldn't get out of bed.
The hands on the clock never moved.
I lay there and stared the whole afternoon.

Have You Ever?

Have you ever felt alone while amidst in a crowd?
Or have you ever had to whisper
Cause you were afraid to speak out loud
Were you ever made to feel different
Because of the shape of your eyes,
The texture of your hair
Or the color of your skin?
Was trying to survive in this society
A battle you just could not win?
Have you ever felt the wrongness of what was really right?
Or were you ever so fed up with the system
You wanted to stand up and fight back?
Have you ever been denied a reason based only on a "because"?
Have you ever had the urge to hate something or someone?
Did you ever have to leave when you had no place to go?
Have you ever said yes, when you felt the answer was no?
Have you ever prayed in the middle of the day?
And thanked God for giving you just one more day
"Have you ever?"

A Dozen Red Roses

Four words whispered through my ears
Ever so soft and faint, comforting yet protective
As if spoken by a saint. "I'll always love you!"
Look in my eyes and tell me you don't see.
The way my eyes light up when you look at me.
Truth of the matter. I know how you feel.
We are both married to other people
Therefore our fantasy can never be real.
I can see it in your eyes when you look at me.
I quickly turn away to keep you from seeing what I see.
Through tear-stained eyes I looked at him
We both knew what the outcome had to be.
By no means was this easy,
But we both knew from the start
The price we would pay,
For stealing each other's heart.

He sent me a dozen red roses the other day
He apologized for loving me
Then he turned and walked away.

Home Without You

Dedicated to Michael

I never thought how lonely I would be,
If God decided to take you from me.
The first night I left you in AICU,
I felt so helpless; there was nothing I could do.
So I decided to leave you in God's hand.
I knew he would take care of you.
Still I prayed all night, it gave me peace of mind.
The next day you were sent to SICU
You had excessive pain the whole night through.
I know how you felt, cause I felt your pain.
I yelled for your nurse to give you something for pain.
"He just had pain med, he's not due again!"
So I held your hand, there was nothing else I could do.
By the time I got home, and kicked off my shoes.
I finally realized, "I was home without you!"

Homeless with Keys

On my way home from work one day
I saw a homeless man
Standing in the entrance way.
Hesitantly I asked if anything was wrong.
He looked at me then proceeded on.
I slowly walked behind him,
He was homeless man. He didn't belong in here.
He took out some keys and unlocked an apartment door.
He went inside as though he's been there before.
The next morning as I was leaving for work.
I saw the same homeless man, dressed in a dark blue suit.
He wasn't always homeless living on the streets.
He lived in Dixx Hills, had a good job, he was
Married twice with three kids and a dog.
His wife left him and took the three kids.
Six months later he lost his job and his Benz.
The rest is history; he ended up homeless on the streets.
Going from shelter to shelter
Eating food from the streets.
Now when I see a homeless man on the street.
I nod and wonder, "Does he have a set of keys?"

Odium

I hated you for such a very long time
I had to learn to forgive.
This hatred was messing up my mind.
I tried to stick by you through thick and thin.
After a while we stopped being friends.
Without being friends, our love never had a chance.
Our relationship was lost; it was a thing of the past.
I hated you for such a long time
I forgot how to smile; I only knew how to frown.
Emotionally you stripped me of everything I had.
After a while my love finally died.
I was afraid to leave, and afraid to stay.
This wasn't a real marriage, there had to be a better way.
There was only one thing left to do
I packed up my kids and told you we were through.
It's been twenty years since I walked out on you.
I never looked back, sad, but true.

Relaxation

This year my life has really been a mess.

They say relaxation is the best cure for stress.

I don't always have time to unwind after work.

I stopped drinking and smoking two years after my stroke.

I don't want a heart attack or chronic anxiety.

I have to learn to relax to live happily ever after.

I'm pulled in too many different directions.

My time schedule consists of twenty-four/seven.

I have to lessen the toll on my body and mind.

I should take this advice

If I want to be around for a while.

"Stop struggling and accept the situation at hand"

This sounds like a winner, it sounds like a plan.

I tried some things to help me relax,

Like jogging, yoga, and a little Prozac.

They say relaxation is the best cure for stress

I have to learn to relax; I have to take care of myself.

In Memory of Donald

When we were kids, we were always together.
Mom was always working,
And Ronnie was out with the fellers.
We were closer than brother and sister,
We actually were good friends.
Of course we had our fights,
"But that's a sibling thing."
I remember it was a Wednesday night.
You stayed after school to try out for track.
It was getting late, and you hadn't come home.
So I waited by the phone in case you tried to call.
Suddenly I heard a loud knock at the door,
My mother screamed, "Oh, God, not my son!"
My father caught her as she fell to the floor.
There was a terrible accident about two hours before.
My brother was killed
By someone who didn't mean it.
He was crossing the Sunrise highway,
Perhaps not paying attention.
My brother was only fifteen when he died.
God called him to heaven to sit by His side.

Inner Strength

Dedicated to Shawn

You got an attitude
Cause I didn't want to do your hair.
I had so much drama going on that day
Your attitude just didn't seem fair.
I couldn't talk to you about it
We were both having a bad day.
I had so much on my mind
I went to church everyday to pray.
Everything happened at once
It was like a Murphy's Law Day
Nothing that day went right.
I was ready to blow my brains away!
You would have been very proud of me.
I took some advice you once told me.
I sorted all my problems out,
And handled them one by one.
I don't know where all that drama came from
But I was able to find peace of mind.
If I got nothing else from this
I found some inner strength and peace.

It's Not My Job

Girlfriend told me the other night
Her husband had a problem of coming home late at night.
I said to her, "But how can that be,
Aren't you his wife, didn't you teach him?"
"Don't forget," I went on to say,
"Women are the backbone of men today."
Girlfriend blurted out, "That's not my job
I thought I married a man
Not someone's child."
Again I told her, "Men are like little boys
If you don't teach them,
They'll grow up and act wild."
So if your man is running the streets at night.
It's your fault for not teaching him what's right.
Girlfriend said,
"It's not my job to teach him what's right!
I'm not his mother,
I'm just his wife."

Jean Marie Butts

Dedicated to my mother-in-law

I've known you for over twenty years.
Never as a mother-in-law,
But as one of my friends.
Many years before I met you
I was told you had a heart of stone.
And you would never like me
Cause "Jean Marie doesn't like anyone."
I'm glad I didn't prejudge you,
Instead I took my time to know you
Of all the years I've been acquainted with you,
I have yet to see the other side of you.
I love you more than you'll ever know
I hope you see me as your friend
Instead of your daughter-in-law.
As time goes on,
And you may need a friend.
Remember my offer,
And that's to a friend from a friend.

Judge Not

Of all the people we encounter in a day
We tend to make inferences,
To what certain people may do or say.
They say friends are mirrors of ourselves
So think about this when you prejudge someone else.
It's very difficult to know a person in one day
Take time to get to know them,
They may have something of importance to say.
Perception of others and ourselves are similar.
Self-based on past familiarity
And certain lifetime endeavors.
We gather information and try to evaluate others.
Often resorting to stereotyping a sistah or a brother.
We come to know our own feelings and attitudes;
Certain situations put us in
A compassionate or indifferent mood.
Don't judge others by what you take for granted
Or self-based logic on past life experiences.

Just be Friends

Dedicated to Donna

My Mom tried to warn me about you.
I didn't listen; I thought your love was true.
You said all the things I wanted to hear.
I thought it was love,
But your love had a different meaning.
For the past seven months
I've shared my emotions with you.
I let down my wall and allowed you to come through.
I've never asked for more than you could give.
"Baby look into my eyes, my love is for real!"
I knew it was the beginning of my end.
The night you said, "Let's just be friends!"
Now that it's over, I have to admit
Your love wasn't that strong,
I fell in love much too quick.
Mom was right, she knew from the start.
If I gave up love too quickly,
It would eventually break my heart.
The next time around I'll know just what to do.
I'll take my time before I fall in love with you.

Just, Tina

Dedicated to Justina

When I was a little girl, I was very, very shy.
I was tall and skinny, with very large blue eyes.
When I got a little older, my red hair began to curl.
The little boys would say to me,
"Only a mother could love!"
This stigma stuck with me until I was in my teens.
Then like Metamorphous, my appearance began to change.
I turned into this gorgeous butterfly, with long beautiful wings.
Like a bird I left the nest, to experience life on my own.
Guys see me differently now,
Some even say I'm gorgeous and fly.
I'm still the same person I've always been.
"Beauty is only skin deep," I heard from a friend.
So all you guys that used to tease me,
Take a good look to what I turned out to be!

In God's Hands

As I lay in the hospital bed last night.
I had mixed feelings
Of what was wrong and what was right.
The doctor said, "You have to make a decision!"
Tests showed something was wrong with my baby.
If I had the baby, there would be a lot of risks.
There were no guarantees he would survive beyond six.
I could terminate the pregnancy, or leave it in God's hand.
Whatever I decided would affect our lives forever.
My baby would never be a normal kid,
Or play with the other kids.
He would never know I was his mommy
He would lie in his crib and cry for hours.
I asked God to help me make the decision
Could I determinate my babies life because of health reasons?
So I decided to leave it in God's hand
Whatever He decided, I would accept and understand.
My baby was born at two in the morning.
Before I got a chance to name him,
God sent for Him early that next morning.

Keya's First Party

Keya's working part time at Path Mark this summer.
She's working thirty hours,
Making a little spending money.
Her and her friends, Jackie and Kelly
Went shopping to buy something nice for the party.
Keya went to a sweet sixteen party tonight.
The outfit she wore made her daddy real mad.
He comes in the room yelling and screaming.
"How dare she wear that, her body is showing!"
You spend so much time writing that poetry book
You don't take time to see how your daughter looks.
I looked at him and let him talk,
It was okay to blame me for Keya's outfit.
I heard him later as he talked on the phone.
He was laughing and joking like nothing was wrong.
Several times I thought about watching TV with him.
But if he was going to make me feel guilty
"Then to hell with him!"

Killing Me With Lies

Eventually the day will come
I'll have to stop running and face my problems.
I love you with all my heart, but
The lies you tell just break my heart.
We stopped being friends many months ago.
I can learn to forgive,
But the process will be slow.
You lied to me, you had an affair,
This proved to me, how much you cared.
Women beep you all day and all night
Where's the respect, "I'm still your wife!"
People always telling me this and that,
What club they saw you and that woman dancing at.
I'm not superwoman; my heart is not made of steel.
Of course those rumors hurt me,
I don't know what to believe.

Krazy on a Normal Day

For many years I thought I was crazy
But found out society was crazy too.
"So how do you live in a crazy world?"
Who makes up the rules, the guys or the girls?
Who decides what's crazy, who makes up these rules?
Is he really crazy or just acting a fool?
So what seems crazy on a normal day?
I saw an old man walking down the street.
He had on winter clothes;
It was a hundred and five degrees.
And how about the man just acting a fool
It's twenty below zero,
And he's not wearing any clothes.
Or the woman with the baby on her back.
She has no place to live,
Cause she would rather buy crack.
This young couple trying to sell their baby boy.
With the money they get, they plan to buy a new car.
So what seems crazy on a normal day?
Absolutely nothing, society says it's ok.

Don't Forget to Leave My Keys

You asked to borrow my sister's car
You wanted to look for a part-time job.
You didn't come back till three days later
Bull S... I said, you weren't with your brother Taylor.
You sweet talked me and I let you back in,
You promised you would do better.
A piece of paper fell from your jacket
It was a brief note signed, "love Heather"
They say love is blind, but I'm beginning to see.
If you want dinner tonight,
You better go and buy the food.
The next time you tell me this baby ain't yours
Your stuff will be packed, waiting for you at the door.
It's not what I can do for you, the question is
"What can you do for me?"
If you can't see where I'm coming from
Maybe it's best that you leave.
As he turned to leave, I whispered,
"Don't forget to leave my door key!"

Laughter is Good

Dedicated to Nadine

Girlfriend told me something the other day.
That caused her to feel angry and very sad.
The way she expressed it, I found myself laughing.
She continued to talk trying to release her pain.
The more she talked,
The more I was doubled over with pain.
She looked at me with a serious look on her face.
"My feelings are hurt, get that smile off your face!"
She told me some stuff that really pissed her off.
I was laughing so hard I started to cough.
I continued to listen because I'm a good friend.
But before I knew it, I was laughing again.
She told me something about our friend Bert.
The way she expressed it, it sounded like a joke.
Just then we both began to laugh,
Tears poured from our eyes, like water from a glass.
Girlfriend, I said with a serious look on my face,
It can't be that serious, if we both can laugh like this.

Life is no Dress Rehearsal

Don't waste your time dreaming of things to come.
You can make things happen, for once and for all.
Don't waste your time holding on to the past.
Get on with your life and stop wasting precious time.
It's not whether it's black or it's white
The question's not based on it being wrong or right.
It's not what you perceive to be true.
It's not lying and pretending it's the truth.
Christ was the only one that died and came back.
So after death we have to assume this is it!
Enjoy life today, cause it can all be taken away.
Don't worry about things when you have no control.
Too much time is wasted, putting your life on hold.
Make each day count, cause when it's all over
God doesn't want to hear any of your sad stories.

Liquid Sunshine

You can't enter the future
If your heart is still buried in the past.
Your life could be so much better
But you have to let the anger pass.
Whatever it takes to make you happy.
Or make your life whole and complete.
Look within your soul,
There you will find inner peace.
Instead of seeing the glass half empty
You'll see the glass as being half full.
Remember to take one day at a time.
Instead of seeing rain,
You'll see liquid sunshine.
Take off those rose colored glasses
And see life as it really is.
No one promised you a rose garden
It's up to you how you choose to feel.

Love Shouldn't Hurt

You say you love me, but how can that be.
When we are home together,
You're reading a book or watching TV.
You know what really bothers me,
When you're in the streets till two am.
Love shouldn't hurt the way that it does.
We do more fighting than making love.
You look me straight in my face
And tell me a lie with a grin on your face.
I've outgrown you, it can happen you know.
It takes two to make a relationship work
And two to make it go wrong.
I've been telling you
The relationship isn't working.
I've been unhappy for so long
It ain't even funny.
Love's not supposed to hurt this way.
I can't make you change,
And you can't make me stay.

Make My Day

There are certain things that make my day.
It makes me feel good on a really bad day.
I like a clean house, and my bed always made.
And everything in order,
"Remember you're getting paid."
Please don't leave the dirty dishes in the sink.
We'll get ants and roaches, I'm sure you don't want this!
Do your homework without being told
And if it's not too much trouble,
Pick up your dirty clothes.
I don't like you fighting with your little brother
He's only seven, why do you treat him so mean?
Give the kid a break; don't make me tell you again!
"Didn't you hear what I just said?"
No, go ahead, make my day!

Mama Got a Bad Habit

Dedicated to Lera

I picked up a bad habit nearly fifty years ago.
Now I'm in respiratory distress,
My lungs don't work anymore.
I was down to two packs of cigarettes a day.
I tried to go cold turkey, but that didn't work.
I even tried the Nicotine patch, what a joke!
I'm walking around with a O_2 tank;
I have no one to blame, only myself to thank.
I can go without a cigarette maybe a day
Then my head gets dizzy, my mind goes astray.
Ronnie and Deb are really mean to me
They won't buy me cigarettes,
"Can you believe them?"
I have to die of something, that's my excuse.
Still they refuse to get me cigarettes
"Isn't that parent abuse?"

Mama's Crazy

Mama's crazy, but you didn't hear it from me.

She has quite a few different personalities.

Don't get me wrong; she'll give you the shirt off her back.

Before the week is over,

She's expecting that same shirt back.

Mama's specialty is mending broken hearts.

Mama will help anyone under the sun,

Especially if the damage was done by her only son.

Sometimes Mama talks to herself,

I really I don't know how true.

Any advice she gives,

You can count on it as being the truth.

My dad looks at Mama and just shakes his head.

Sometimes he can't believe what's coming out of her head.

Mama's crazy, but it's nothing new.

She interrupts dreams, and analyzes pictures too.

Mama tells folks to unlock childhood memories,

She teaches them to swim above the rain.

She'll listen to your problems all day,

Is she crazy or sane?

Many Thanks to You

Dedicated to the Staff at Stony Brook Hospital

I had a paroxysm a couple of weeks ago.
My wife forced me to see Dr. Newman and Dr. Bernal.
She said she trusted them with the welfare of her man.
Tests showed something serious was wrong.
I took an x-ray, MRI, and a CT with injectable dye.
Dr. Manzione, I heard was the best,
Was going to use his expertise to correct this mess.
Susan Aiello was great, you know
She answered all of my questions, with a simple yes or no.
Surgery went well, the operation was a success.
Several weeks from now, I'll be back to myself.
Dr. R. Davis cut into my brain, while Rick A.
Made sure everything went according to plan.
Donna came by to make sure everything was all right.
Norma (18N) pulled out my Foley; I think I saw stars that night.
Patty Westgate came by that Sunday
And while talking to my wife,
She calmly cut something from my neck with a knife.
In fourteen days the staples will be removed.
I'll grow some hair to hide my horseshoe.
Here's to the staff at Stony Brook Hospital.
Thanks to the hard work you did,
"I'm feeling much better!"

Migraine

There is nothing worse than a migraine.
It's the worst pain you could ever imagine.
I took imitrex when it first began.
Still no relief, my head is still hurting.
I took more medication about two hours ago.
My head feels like it wants to explode.
I can't function when my head hurts like this.
I'm very sensitive to light, noise and scents.
I can't wait for tomorrow to come
I'll be back to myself cause the migraine will be gone.
This migraine will be the death of me yet.
When I'm in pain like this
I just want to shoot myself.
Since I know what causes my migraine,
I try to stay away from those factoring things.
But sometimes I can't and I'm forced play the game
The aggravation of another Migraine.

Mothers, Teach Your Sons

The mother compares him to his father
Therefore he will never be a strong man.
I wonder if you mothers realize
The damage you do to your young men.
A son is only what his mother allows him to be.
If that mother doesn't take pride in her son
It's a pity what that son will grow up to be.
He'll spend his life taking care of his mother's needs.
Only to find nothing will ever please her.
In order to survive, he moves out
And leaves his mother's side.
He marries a woman just like his mom,
Chances are she won't love him enough
And will end up doing him more harm.
So now he's married with two boys of his own.
He teaches them values and how to be strong men.
His mother taught him to hold everything inside.
He teaches his sons, it's ok if you have to cry.
He no longer blames his mother for the past.
Sometimes he thinks about his childhood
And tries to forget the damage that was done.

Moving Again

Dedicated to Kim

If I have to move just one more time.
Please lock me up,
Cause I'm going to be out of my mind.
I have moved seven times in the past three years.
I'm so tired of moving, I'm having nightmares!
As soon as I get settled and call the place home,
The landlord sells it, and I have to move on.
My stuff is still packed from the last time I moved.
I have unpacked boxes all over my room.
Now I'm waiting to buy my own house.
But before I do that, I have to move back home.
Don't get me wrong, my family is great!
Just the thought of living home again
Gives me anxiety attacks!
Terrance thinks it's great
Living with Grandpa and Grandma.
Everyday is Friday,
And he doesn't have to do any chores.
Hakeem and his boys are going to help me again.
"I just don't like moving, it's not my thing!"

Melting Pot of Love

People stare at us when we walk down the street.

We are just holding hands.

We're in love; it's not a secret.

I feel proud when I'm walking by your side.

You are very special, and you're one of a kind.

Society feels we should stay with our own kind.

But who is society, and why do they make these rules?

How dare they tell me what I can and cannot do?

I love you for all the right reasons.

When society sees us together,

You'd think we've committed some kind of treason.

When I look at you, I see a happy ending.

Society says it's a black and white thing.

"Think of your children, they will be different, not the same."

Don't they realize love is a big melting pot?

And when you stir all the ingredients together.

Love is what it is all about!

My Garden

I sit in my garden each and every day.
And write down my thoughts of what happened that day.
Putting my emotions on paper, trying to get my feelings out
Relaxing in my garden, helps me to express my inner thoughts.
It helps me understand what life is all about.
Instead of wasting time
Trying to figure the impossible things out.
I planted my garden many years ago.
My positive thoughts make my flowers grow.
I have inner peace when I sit in my garden
This atmosphere is serene, secure and relaxing.
Here I have a clear conscience
And little things don't matter.
I always take time to smell my flowers.
I enjoy life more, cause now I have a purpose.
Come visit my garden whenever you can.
It's peaceful here, you can relax and unwind.
We'll have a cup of tea, perhaps a glass of wine.
We can enjoy my garden, or express what's on your mind.
My message to you, "Enjoy the rain and the sunshine."

My New Baby Brother

I still don't know what all this talk is about.
Mommy ate something that made her belly stick out.
Mommy and Daddy talk to her belly every night.
She asked me one night,
"You want to tell your brother goodnight?"
I looked at her, then I looked at my daddy.
"I don't understand all this talk about her belly."
Mommy talks to her belly to make it grow.
She said inside was a baby with fingers and toes!
This scared me, so I ran to my room.
"No baby like that is going to share my room!"
The day finally came my baby brother was born.
I stole a peek when he was in my mommy's arms.
I remember Mommy said it had fingers and toes.
But when I looked closely, I saw two eyes and a nose.
Maybe this baby thing won't be so bad,
It looks like me and a little like my dad.
I guess I can share my room with him
He's my baby brother, and I have to protect him.

My Thoughts

On quiet days I sit and think
Maybe a little more than I should.
Sometimes I'm scared to trust my thoughts;
My thoughts sometime control my moods.
I can sit for hours and not have anything to say.
Sometimes I'm afraid to tell you who I am
Maybe you will judge me,
Or simply won't understand.
I choose to be alone with my thoughts.
I don't have to explain what I am thinking about.
My thoughts are my own;
There I have nothing to hide.
Sometimes negative thoughts try to enter my head.
The same answer repeats, "You don't have to be afraid!"
I wish I didn't care so much
I'm more caring than strangers ever know.
And if by chance I try to hide
My true feelings I keep inside.
I wonder, will you understand?
My thoughts are my reality...

My Three Sons

Dedicated to Sue Z Q

To my first son, I've always loved you best.
You were my dreamer,
Your head was always in the clouds.
You grew to be a handsome young man.
You have made me very, very proud.

True, you owe me lots of money,
Maybe one day you might pay me back.
But all in all, we are family,
And I'll always have your back.

To my second son, I've always loved you best.
Your smile brightens up my darkest day,
You loan me money on my off paydays
You're always trying to help Scott out,
I'm proud you understand what family is all about.

To my third son, I've always loved you best.
I never thought the day would come.
You would be off to college to live on your own.
When it's time to say goodbye,
I'll turn my head so you won't see me cry.

Enter Manhood

I raised you three boys the best I knew how.
I guess I did a good job,
You all have made me very proud.
I tried to give you everything I could.
There were many times
I went without something new
I worked very hard day in and day out.
To give you things, I only dreamed about.
I never had a mother who stuck by me,
But you better believe I stuck by you three.
There were many times when Allen got mad
I got between you to save your a...!
I know it seems that your father doesn't care.
His heart is full of sorrow and despair.
You three boys have been my life,
Now let me stand back,
So you can start living your own life.

Mythology of Color

There is no scientific poof
That color has anything to do with one's intelligence.
They say I'm black but my skin is brown.
I looked Black up in Webster's dictionary
And this is what I found:
     Black is evil
      Wicked
       Soiled
        Angry
         Dirty
          Cheerless
           Depressing
           Gloomy
I thought to myself as I read this out loud,
Is that how they see me, not black and not proud?
I knew Webster must have made a mistake,
Those words weren't true, that dictionary was fake!
         Black comedy
          Black death
           Black guard
            Black ball
             Black list
Black is beautiful, I'm black and I'm proud.
That stuff Webster wrote should be banned or outlawed.
There is no scientific proof that color has anything to do
With one's intelligence.

Nappy Hair

My Grandma called me her nappy-head little girl.
You would think it was my fault
I was born with naps instead of curls.
I hated when Grandma combed my hair
She would pull and stretch it, like she didn't even care.
Now don't let me cry when Grandma combed out my naps.
Cause when I pulled forward,
She would snap my head back.
When Grandma got my naps all under control,
She made me get the hot comb,
I guess to punish me some more!
"Now, Baby Girl, sit still," Grandma would always say.
This hot comb will make your hair nice and pretty!
Why is she blaming me cause my hair's nappy.
Did she forget who was my mommy and who was my daddy?
After my hair was all nice and shiny,
"Come here baby girl,"
Let Grandma see her little princess!

Never Meant to Hurt You

You may not believe this,
But I never meant to hurt you, or make you cry.
I think you have failed to realize
My heart was broken too.
The difference is, I choose to survive.
Sometimes it bothers me
You think my heart is made of steel.
I'm just an average black man
I just refuse to wear my heart on my sleeve.
When we first met,
I laid all my cards on the table.
I tried to be totally honest with you,
I just never told you all the facts that were true.
During the time of our relationship
I tried very hard to be faithful to you.
When the relationship was over
I had to make a new start.
I did my crying on rainy days
When the rain finally stopped,
I decided to change my ways.

No Hidden Message

Dedicated to E. Joseph

You've been studying the stars
As long as I can remember.
You have lived half of your life
Still you look melancholic and miserable.
You have the same dreams you had before.
Nothing new and nothing to show for.
You've made big mistakes raising your sons.
They don't respect you, they were taught all wrong.
Sometimes I wonder why our paths ever met
I know it was meant to happen,
Regardless of our past regrets.
I don't wish anything ill of you
I wish you nothing but happiness, "It's true!"
I hope you find in life whatever you are searching for.
The past has already happened
There's no need for me to be angry anymore.
Your journey through life has been very arduous
I hope you find inner peace, through past life experiences.

Of All Things to Lose

Dedicated to Jean Marie

I don't remember as well as before.
My memory fails me, why, I don't know.
The other day I forgot to lock my door.
A stranger came in and robbed my house.
What if I forget to feed my cat?
Or take a walk, and forget my way back.
Suppose I forget to take my pills or
Forget I am sick and become seriously ill.
I don't remember as well as before.
My memory fails me, why, I don't know.
Suppose my daughter-in-law came to visit
And I forgot her name; this would be so hurtful,
I would feel so ashamed.
Sometimes I forget; this can happen you know.
Of all things to lose, I don't want my memory to go.
I'm going to write down things I don't want to ever forget.
Hernando quick, "Give me a pencil before I forget!"

$$$$$ of Love

I wish I could afford to give you everything you want.
I'm still paying for the stuff I brought you last month.
I wish I could afford to give you the finer things in life.
Already I'm working three full-time jobs at night.
I'm not a rich man, as you well know.
I'm driving a van that's seven years old.
I know you are accustomed to the finer things in life.
What good are those riches
When you are sleeping alone each night?
I sense you are lonely, cause I'm lonely too.
It's a shame we can't get together,
Cause I can't afford you.
Of course I feel bad when I can't take you out to eat.
You always want to go to places
That cost sixty-five dollars a plate.
I don't have anything, sad, but true.
Look beyond the dollar signs,
I'm a fool in love with you.

Old Friends

Dedicated to Marva Wells

Remember when we first met
I was eighteen and three months pregnant.
I think Mr. Hall was the principle at the time.
Had something to do with you coming to my house.
During those months we became very good friends.
Our friendship has lasted throughout all these years.
We don't see each other everyday,
Or talk on the phone to pass the time away.
We often plan to meet for lunch
Something comes up, and then we lose touch.
You always send me a birthday card,
When I open to read it, I just stand there and smile.
A Christmas has never gone by,
You haven't sent me a card, or to just say hi.
So here's to you Mrs. Marva Wells,
I want you to know how much you are thought of.

Pain in a Bottle

If I knew then what I know now
I would have been a better father
I would have known all the answers to "why?"
If I could turn back the hands of time
I would have spent more time being happy,
Instead I waited for things to go wrong.
I couldn't stop living in the past,
I drank everyday while I listened to my jazz.
I hid my emotions very well.
But between you and me,
My life was a living hell.
I continued to drink to hide my true feelings.
Until one day my mind wanted to holler
And my soul wanted to scream.
When I could no longer
Blame my father for my pain.
I turned to alcohol to deaden my feelings.
I drank each day when I came home from work.
I looked for excuses to drink and smoke.
In case you don't know what I am talking about
For fifteen years I was an alcoholic.

Patches

Let me tell you about Patches,
He was one of a kind.
He had spots on his back, with nice brown eyes.
He was a very special dog,
With a mind of his own.
Patches wasn't afraid of any dogs on his block.
He went up to them and barked real loud.
I saw Patches once in a Pit bull's face.
I did all I could to pull Patches away.
The other dog looked surprised and shocked.
But you have to admit, Patches had a lot of heart.
Patches was special in his own right.
The more Eric tried to keep him in the house
The more Patches ran the streets at night.
Before daylight Patches would always come back home
To sit in his front yard, protecting his surroundings.

Phone Call to Dad

"Hi Dad, it's me again.
I have a few problems,
You got a few minutes to listen?
I don't like to bother you with my personal life.
But when I talk with Mom, she makes me think twice.
My marriage is so confusing, to say the least.
I have everything I want; yet something serious is missing.
Now don't get me wrong, I'm well provided for.
I just need my husband to be home a little more.
I know he loves to hang out with the boys.
Then he doesn't come home till three o'clock or four.
I thought about leaving many times before.
He talks me into staying, promises to try a little more.
Dad, Erick just got home, so I have to go.
He's taking me to New York, to see a Broadway Show.
Daddy, thank you for listening, I'll call you next Sunday.
Tell Mom she was right, I was feeling a little lonely."

Please Let Me Go

We've been married for over sixty years
Cancer has taken away my desire to live.
I suffer with pain each and everyday.
The morphine they give me does nothing these days.
My husband sits beside me, telling me to hold on.
"Hold on to what, my life is all gone!"
The pain is so intense I can't take it anymore.
I'm only holding on,
Cause my husband won't let go.
I ask God every morning I wake up.
"How much longer do I have to go through this stuff?"
Can't God see I've suffered enough?
I'm almost eighty-three, I've lived enough.
I've lived a good life all of these years.
I'm ready to go now...please!

Present Moments

There were many hearts I've broken on the way
You must believe me; I didn't plan it that way.
I never meant to break your heart and make you cry.
When all of this is over,
You'll thank me for telling you goodbye.
Cause it's hard for one to get ahead
When there is dead weight around her legs.
Very often she'll forget about her goals in life
And settle for a husband working at McDonald's at night.
So dry your eyes and please don't cry.
What we had together was not based on lies.
Everything happened for a reason.
Even the cheating and the lies.
It was up to me to call it quits,
I couldn't stand to see you cry.
We enjoyed present moments
So now let's kiss and say goodbye.

Punishment

Dedicated to Keya

Sitting in my room
Staring at the calendar on the wall.
How many more days,
Do I have to stare at these walls?
Who invented this thing called punishment?
Must have been an adult
Cause no kid I know
Would have thought up this stuff.
I stay on punishment for weeks on end.
I can't remember the last time
I spoke to Jackie on the phone.
I never have fun anymore,
My whole life is in ruin,
"OK, it was my fault for acting up in school."
Dad took away everything in my room.
No television or radio, he unplugged my telephone.
I'm only allowed out to eat and to shower.
Then return to my room within the next hour.
I haven't been out of this house for three months.
This punishment stuff ain't no joke.

Questioning My Love

Don't you know I would never hurt you
Or deliberately make you cry?
Now you're questioning my love for you
Cause something happened and you think I lied.
Regardless of what your friends had to say,
The incident really didn't happen that way.
I was at the right place at the wrong time,
Ran into an old friend.
We talked and had a glass of wine.
I said goodbye and kissed her on the cheek.
Went straight to your place, then we went out to eat.
I don't know what your friends thought they saw.
But I'm disappointed in you for believing their lies.
I've always been faithful and honest with you.
You asked me what went down and I told you the truth.
I don't know what else you want me to say.
I swear to you, it didn't happen that way.

The Mighty Quinn

I watched as you moved into the apartment above me.
I could tell from afar,
You had certain qualities.
You were young, buffed and wearing a Gerri curl,
You flashed me a smile that lit up my world.
We read each other's thoughts daily.
It was like unspoken words,
Until we knew we were both ready.
I met you at a crucial time in my life.
You woke up my spirits and brought excitement to my life.
We had a very strange relationship, to say the least.
You held me close, I felt your heart beat.
People may not understand what we did for each other.
But it was quite normal between a woman and her lover.

Rainbows

I saw two rainbows the other night
I knew in my heart my life was about to change.
For many years I've put my dreams on hold.
By 2001, I plan to reach all of my goals.
The first I'll do is gather up my thoughts.
Put them down on paper,
And write my heart out.
I'll paint a mental picture
Of what I want to come true.
Cause at this point in my life,
There's nothing I can't do.
Maybe I'll finish my novel,
Perhaps I'll write a poetry book or two.
The sky is the limit,
Cause there's nothing I can't do.

Rather be Alone

Dinner was ready twenty minutes ago.
I lit some candles and waited for you.
I sat and waited till almost midnight
I felt frightened; you were never out this late.
I thought for sure something had happened to you.
I waited and waited the whole night through.
When I heard your key turn in the door,
I quickly jumped up and went to meet you at the door.
You reeked of liquor, and smelled like some cheap whore.
I packed your things and asked you to leave.
I have no intentions of taking this emotional abuse.
You promised to be faithful,
And begged for another chance.
The same thing happened three months later.
I don't need E.S.P. to know you've been unfaithful.
So I'll tell you what I'm going to do.
I'll give you your freedom
So you can do what the hell you want to do.

Rebirth of a Woman

I look within my isolated heart
Through my crumbled walls of despair.
And thank God I got out of that relationship
Cause after awhile he no longer cared.
I close my eyes and thank God,
That I opened my eyes in time.
I tried to bake him a cake with humility,
And a smile to quench his thirst.
A vow to love him forever,
With pure honesty and everlasting trust.
My jaws are clinched so tightly,
That my gums began to bleed.
My screams echo through the rubbles
As I drop on to my knees.
I quickly turn to my man.
His eyes were blinded by his own fixes and needs.
I put my right hand on my chest,
And I could feel my own heart bleed.
It was the first thing I'd blame;
Yet the last thing I would forgive.
I was the essence of his life,
Yet he was afraid to let me live.

Remember Me

Dedicated to Dora

You're only ten months olds
How are you going to remember me?
Or the songs I sang while I rocked you to sleep.
I phoned the other day, I wanted to say hi.
Your mommy said you were taking a nap.
And she'll tell you Grandma called.
My biggest fear is you forgetting me,
I don't want to think of that ever happening.
I love you like my own little girl.
When you laughed, I saw Sammy's smile.
Now that you're gone, I don't know what to do.
The house is so empty; there are no sounds of you.
Your room is so quiet, your stuffed animals must know
Their little girl has gone away, and they won't see her anymore.
I'll come to visit whenever I can, and call you often,
So you won't forget who I am.

Retirement

I've worked hard for over sixty-five years.
Now because of my age,
My company wants me to leave.
They call it Retirement,
For no other better name.
But a rose is a rose by any other name.
I'm in good health,
I've never missed a day of work.
I don't feel sixty-five,
"So why can't I continue to work?"
The office gave me a party, and a nice gold watch.
I held in my tears as I walked away from the office.
At first I was depressed having nothing to do.
Then said to myself, as I sometimes do,
"I'm only sixty-five, my life ain't through!"
Come Monday morning,
I'm going to find me something to do!
Not only did I find me a part-time job,
Mona, the woman down the street,
Is trying to steal my heart.
Then I said to myself, as I sometimes do,
"I'm only sixty-five, my life ain't through!"

Right Thing to Do

Dedicated to Anthony

We got married much to young
We started having babies instead of having fun.
But we stuck it out; we did what we had to do.
But somewhere down the road
You stopped loving me, I stopped loving you.
I couldn't continue to live like this
Our situation was driving me insane.
It's not anyone's fault, we both share the blame.
I have been to hell's kitchen
And cleaned out all of the pots.
Most of the marriage
I was drinking and high off pot.
I never meant to cause you no pain
I got you pregnant, so I just did the right thing.

Running Out of Time

I thought I would never see
Anything worse than the AIDS disease.
Then three years ago
Death claimed my best friend Larry.
He didn't use drugs, and he wasn't gay.
He was going to medical school.
Trying to make a difference in some way.
He had an operation when he was in his teens.
Now he's dying of AIDS
Because of a blood transfusion.
People are dying of AIDS, all over the world.
It doesn't care if you are Black or White.
If you live on Fifth Avenue,
Or if you were raised in Gordon Heights.
AIDS is a horrible life-threatening disease
It's 2001, and we're still searching for answers.
My advice to you "be as careful as you can."
Always use protections
When you're with another woman or another man.

Sasha

1982 - 1999

When Eric and Kim brought you home
You were no bigger than a ball.
You were all black and fluffy
I could barely see you eyes at all.
I tried very hard not to fall in love with you.
But as you grew, you grew on me too.
You were special and very smart.
Sometimes I wondered if you really were a dog.
You listened, you paid attention, and came when we called.
It was hard to believe you really were a dog.
You were never told, but you knew your job.
You protected the home and our kids from all harm.
Though you couldn't speak like humans do,
You wagged your tail when we spoke to you.
You did things no other dog could do
I knew you were special the first time I saw you.

Seven Fathers

I was the only girl raised with seven older brothers.
My brothers picked on me and made me cry.
I was just a little girl, maybe two or three.
But I remember everything my brothers did to me.
My brothers made my life a leaving hell.
I thought for sure I was living in jail.
Very early my brothers taught me to read and write.
How to take care of myself, and even to fight back.
Now I'm older and they are still running my life.
They decide whom I date
And what time to come in on Friday night.
Can you believe my brothers are still running my life?
Now I am married with kids of my own.
Not a day goes by my seven brothers
Don't call me on the phone.
They make sure I am happy, and that nothing is wrong.
You see my father died when I was only three
My seven brothers promised to always take care of me.

Single Mom

"I just can't take it anymore!"
I say over and over again to myself.
Why don't someone help me, I can't do it by myself!
Everyday is a struggle; I do my best to survive.
Life is slowly killing me, and there's no place left to hide.
My car breaks down every other week.
Last month we turned vegetarian,
Cause groceries are cheaper without meat.
I don't have money for school pictures again.
My son needs another haircut, I just can't win!
My TV broke for the third time this month.
The repairman said,
"Miss, it's cheaper to buy a new one!"
I work full time and go to school at night.
I can't win for losing, it just ain't right!
I'm a single mom, don't punish me for that.
Punish the deadbeat dad, who only left his tracks.
I'm just a single mom trying to make ends meet.
While he plays weekend dad with a pizza and two tapes.

Slowly Dying

Each day we are slowly dying
And we're going to be dead for a very long time.
We better get our priorities in order
And stop wasting precious time.
We spend most of our time playing head games
And looking for others than ourselves to blame.
We choose to be unhappy, we choose to be alone.
We swear that life isn't fair,
Then we pretend we just don't care.
Reality can be very painful;
Sometimes the truth hurts a lot.
We find religion, thinking it will make everything all right.
Then reality sets in and the truth comes out.
For once in our life
We see what reality is all about.
This is our reality; this is our heaven and hell.
Get rid of the unnecessary pain,
And start enjoying yourself.
Remember each day we are slowly dying
And we're going to be dead for a very long time...

Society Said

Were you ever taught to hate something or someone?
Well, the fate that brought that fate
Was only the stereotype in which you used to judge others.
You taught your children to hate mine.
Law is for the white man,
Therefore justice is sometime blind.
You use to call me Nigga, and sometimes Black
For hundreds of years
You tried to hold my history back.
You taught me that black was ugly
And my destiny was dammed.
But digit, Black is beautiful and I know who I am.
There was once a time I was totally confused
I lived by the system
And made what society said as my rule.
I straightened my hair to look like the white woman
I denied my blackness and lived in shame,
After all, I was a black woman
Trying to play the white man's game.

Solitude

I went outside to finish reading my book.

My husband said, "Babe, are you going to cook?"

I looked at him, then I closed my book,

And this is what I said,

"You have to give me a minute,

I just got home from work.

I need a little space,

Is that asking for too much?"

Solitude is not a luxury, it is my given right.

Sometimes I need to have my own space,

Even if you don't think it's right.

When I go away from you,

I'm not being selfish.

I just need some time from you

To make myself feel better.

So Sweetheart, if you don't mind,

Please get me a chilled glass of white wine.

And as soon as I finish my book,

I'll come inside and cook.

Something is Missing

I wish I knew what I was looking for.
Cause maybe I have it and just don't know.
I have a good husband, and a fine little boy.
We have our own business, a grocery store.
Still something is missing, I still have this void.
Sometimes I feel angry for no reason at all.
By the time you come home,
I'm callous and uncaring.
Maybe that's the reason I can't get your attention.
I thought the new house would bring us closer together.
We still have the same drama;
We can't seem to get it together.
I know you love me in your own special way.
But it's not enough, it's not okay.
I need more than you are capable of giving
Can't you see something serious is missing?

Someone to Listen

You have opened up my heart
I've shared my feelings with you.
You introduced me to emotions,
 I never before knew.
You said to trust you
With all my emotional feelings.
In time I would get over this harrowing feeling.
I've carried this baggage
As far back as I can remember,
It's time to let go; my back's getting weaker.
I know the answers won't come overnight.
I'm willing to work hard, even to sacrifice.
Thanks for taking the time to listen
It's been six weeks,
Already I can feel a big difference.

Still We're Family

Dedicated to my family

We are all different from one another.
True we don't always act like sisters and brothers
...but we are family.
True we don't visit each other that often.
But if there's ever a crisis,
You can always count on someone to come running.
We have had our bouts of ups and downs,
Somehow it made us stronger for the next go round.
There are three sisters, Dorothy, Lera and Myrtle.
They do what they can to keep the family united
...cause we are family.
Maybe we don't say I love you quite often enough
Or give out hugs when life really gets tough
Or call on birthdays or special events
Or visit the hospital when someone is sick.
We don't visit or call each other that often
...but we're still family
And that has to count for something.

Street Wise

Instead of going to school, I hung in the streets all day.
I had a new family, the streets became my home.
For many years that was the only life I've ever known.
Yea, I run the streets day in and day out.
That's how I make my living,
That's what I'm all about.
Don't act like all this is new, don't forget.
I was in the streets when I met you.
One day a right deal went wrong,
I went up state and made some time.
I can't be what you want me to be.
I was raised in the streets; that's my true identity.
All we seem to do is fuss and fight.
That happens when you force me to do right.
Why can't you understand?
I was raised in the streets, the street is my home.

Terrible Two's

My little girl will turn two today,
Lord, have mercy, is all I can say.
She learned to walk when she was nine months old
She was talking on the phone just like she was grown
She had a full set of teeth before she was one.
I fed her Captain Crunch cereal,
And she ate chicken off the bone.
My little girl was toilet trained before she was one
The older folks listened to her as if she was grown.
I heard her tell her grandma the other day.
She would rather have Pepsi instead of Coke any day.
Everything was why, and how come,
Give me this and leave me alone.
Yes, my little girl will turn two today
Lord, have mercy, is all I can say!

The Playground

I noticed this young girl at the playground today.
She stood quietly in the background
Watching this little boy play.
The way her eyes were protecting him,
I thought for sure she was his mommy.
I saw the same girl at the playground today.
Again she was watching the little boy play.
I noticed something I didn't notice before.
The young girl has red hair, just like the little boy.
I saw the young girl at the playground today.
She was sitting alone with a sad look on her face.
I asked her about the little red head boy.
She said she gave him up
Three weeks after he was born.
She was on drugs, living on the streets
Selling her body to get the next fix.
The young girl said she was unhappy and sad
Cause she could never see her son grow to become a man.
As she told me this story, I looked at her without any pity
"Sorry if I can't show you any compassion,
But you're responsible for your own actions!"

Thou Shalt Not Lie

Either I leave or decide to stay.

It sounds very simple, it's not all that complicated.

Over the years you've changed so much.

You lied and cheated, this makes me not trust.

Lies flow so smoothly from your lips.

You lie about stuff that don't make any sense.

There are only two choices you have to make.

Either get your act together, or pack up and vacate!

You've lied so much, I don't trust you anymore.

When you come home late, I just look at you.

I don't ask where you've been

Cause you won't tell me the truth.

I asked you the other day if you truly loved me.

You looked in my face and stood very still.

Baby, you know I love you with all my heart.

"You know how I feel, my love is that strong!"

Were you telling me the truth or was that, too, a lie?

True or False

I took an emotional quiz the other day
I only answered questions I knew would be safe.
It was easy enough, just true or false.
But I failed the test, cause I was thinking with my heart.
Most of the time I will trust
Until you give me reason to doubt.
I treat people like I want to be treated.
If you ever betray my trust,
I swear, "I'll treat you like an enemy!"
I seldom lie; it defeats the whole purpose,
You can count on me
"Cause my friendship is worth it."
My word is my bond, I give it cautiously.
I'm one of a kind,
You'll know it when you meet me.

Unlock Childhood Memories

There is nothing I can do about the past.
I still have empty voids and angry feelings.
My mom is teaching me how to swim above the rain.
In time I will learn how to live with this pain.
It's a very slow process, but I have time on my side.
I will start from the beginning to uncover my feelings.
I exposed some pain from a long time ago,
It brought tears to my eyes,
The pain was devastating.
Some memories were ugly,
Those I buried real deep.
Once the pain is all out,
My life will be complete.
I'll be able to think with a very clear mind.
Whatever I am or ever hope to be,
My childhood memories played a part in it.
I can't change what has happened in my life.
But now I can see it through grown up eyes.

Until it Has to End

I knew you were married when we first met.
That should have put an end to it all.
After several months of being your friend
I couldn't stop what was in my heart.
I really tried not to fall in love with you.
The more I tried,
The more my heart sought after you.
Then it was that first kiss,
One thing led to another.
Before I realized it,
We had become secret lovers.
We spent stolen moments every chance we got.
We parked our cars
And took long walks in the park
We spent nights just holding each other in the dark.
Early on Sunday morning
We went jogging in Central Park.
I don't know what tomorrow will bring
So I'll enjoy each and every moment
Until this has to end.

Until Tomorrow

Today wasn't perfect
Tomorrow may not be any better.
Poor me, I said to myself
As I turned to watch Jerry Springer.
What's that old saying?
"If it's not one thing it's another."
Or was it, "He's not heavy, he's my brother!"
Little things are upsetting me lately.
My emotions are taking a beating
I don't know what else to say.
Life is so perplexed; there has to be a better way.
If I can just hold on till tomorrow,
I know it will be a better day.

Vietnam

Sending a letter with an upside down stamp.
To a far away soldier in a far away camp.
Spending the day writing love letters and poems.
Promising to be faithful, until you return home.
I put my life on hold waiting for you.
Your letters told me you were waiting too.
It's been three years since you went away.
I counted each moment, I counted each day.
When you returned something has changed.
You weren't the same person; I noticed it right away.
The Vietnam War took something from your strive.
Your soul was now empty, your heart somehow died.
You began to hear voices, you began to drink.
You couldn't forget the war; it was buried too deep.
We were talking one night, something inside you snapped!
You put a gun to my head before reality came back.
I knew you were sorry, it wasn't your fault.
Vietnam had taken away your mind and your thoughts.

War or Peace

I don't want to leave
But you haven't given me any reason to stay
You don't want to change
And I can't go on this way.
You haven't touched my emotions in a very long time.
What I need from you is not this new house.
I don't want black diamonds or white pearls.
I just want you include me in your world.
We can spend an entire day together,
And have nothing to say.
You've hurt me more than I could ever say.
I have to get out of this relationship
I don't want to fight any more.
If you ever really loved me, do me a favor;
And don't bring our son into our war.

Waiting for You

I was aimlessly walking through Smith Haven Mall
Not a care in the world, just messing around.
My eyes straight ahead, my head held high.
Not even wearing a smile, not even wondering why.
My kids were away, I had nothing to do.
My love life was in shambles.
My heart was broken in two.
Then I noticed this man,
Just following me around the mall.
I stole a quick glance at him,
He was looking me up and down.
After awhile I got tired of the chase.
I went up to him and confronted him face to face.
He introduced himself as Mike,
He worked someplace in Hempstead
And attended NYU at night.
He said he had seen me around, he knew I had two kids
That I drove a tan firebird,
And the brother knew exactly where I lived.
His goal was to meet me and get my attention;
Let me say one thing: the brother had determination!

Whiter Shade of Pale

My skin was as white as could be,
It was easy to hide my true identity.
If the truth ever came out, it would be my ending.
How I pass for white and treated black as my enemy.
As black I was treated like I didn't have any rights.
So I moved across town and passed for white.
At eighteen I went to college, and met a good white man.
"Who knew years later he would belong to the Ku Klux Klan?"
His name was Nathan; we dated for three years.
After graduation he wanted to make our fantasy real.
Nathan wanted to get married and have lots of kids.
I did everything I could, so I wouldn't have any babies.
Accidentally I got pregnant; I had to tell Nathan the truth.
To make a long story short, baby Nathan has blue eyes too.

Why Can't They Understand?

I know I'm driving my kids crazy
And perhaps my husband to drink.
Why can't they understand?
I just want them to put things back.
They say I put too much emphasis
On what they should and should not do.
Why can't they understand?
I just want them to be perfect too.
I need to have everything in order,
Is that asking for too much?
When you finish with the toothpaste
Just screw back on the top.
When you finish eating dinner,
Don't just leave your plate there.
Put them in the dishwasher; "Am I the only one who cares?"
Don't forget your dirty clothes, why leave them on the floor.
Just put them in the hamper, or hang them on the door.

Will You Marry Me?

My boyfriend asked me the other night.
I want to put a ring on your finger,
And make love to you to all night.
I promise to make you happy,
And I'll always treat you right.
"I don't think so," I said to him.
How are you going to buy me a ring?
You don't have a job, and I'm still a virgin!
I promise to get a job, and I'll work real hard.
You won't ever have to work; I'll make you very proud.
I don't think so, I said to him.
You need a job before you can get my attention.
So he got a job, and bought my ring.
We later got married, so forth and so on.
To make a long story short, he couldn't keep a job.
He had a problem taking orders, and he often got fired.
Most of the time he would quit his job
With no unemployment;
I had to find a full time job.
We got behind in the rent; I had to move back home.
That's what I get,
For marrying a man with no steady income!

Yo Marijuana!

A friend introduced me to one of his friends;
Her name was Marijuana.
I was told she made exciting things happen.
Once you meet her, your life won't ever be the same.
She'll take you places you've never seen.
This trip sounded interesting, I was ready to go!
I was only seventeen, what the hell did I know.
They say Marijuana's been around for a while.
Until I met her, my life was uninteresting and dull.
The music was jammin'; the food was slammin'
I saw life in a whole different way.
Yo Marijuana, come back this way!
Marijuana introduced me to one of her friends;
Her name was Angel Dust.
She was in town for the weekend.
First I thought I was in heaven;
Within seconds I went straight to hell.
I started hallucinating, then I started to scream and yell.
To make a long story short
I said goodbye to Marijuana and Angel,
Friends like that can only lead to danger!

You and Me

Fate or destiny, it's really out of our hands
Whatever is meant to be, will eventually happen.
As I walked through the room I felt tension, not ease.
I couldn't decide if I wanted to be there or not,
My mind said go, but my heart said stop.
My mind and my heart were having mixed feelings.
I knew I had to make the final decision.
You see my problem is not a simple one.
And the solution has not been found.
My heart is torn between two men.
I'm in a contest I will never be able to win.
I suddenly turned to my lover, his heart was trapped
By my own illusion. I had to finally realize
We had come to the end of our conclusion.
By no means was this easy, but we both knew from the start.
The price we would pay for stealing each other's heart.

You've Changed

Dedicated to Ronda

When you left to go upstate
I visited you faithfully every other week.
I stood by you in your time of need
This went on for many, many years.
Then the tables turned,
I needed you by my side.
I was pregnant with your child
And you were no place to be found.
While I carried your child, all I did was cry.
You didn't seem to care enough,
"I don't know why?"
I can't make you be a father or do what is right.
It has to come from within, otherwise it won't be right.
Sure you get a lot of slack from my family.
And yes, my mother would shoot you on sight!
But they are just concerned for my welfare.
And they want you to do what's right.
We make up to break up; it's part of our routine.
I wonder if you realize how much you are hurting me...

Write a Happy Ending

Dedicated to Kimberly

Why can't you write something cheerful and alive?
My daughter asked me one day.
Why don't you write a happy ending?
Like rainbows, blue skies and sunsets.
Instead you write poems that make people cry.
The stuff you write is depressing and sad
Can't you write a happy ending instead?
"I write about reality, true events in people's lives.
A woman caught cheating, a husband telling lies.
Releasing emotional pain, learning to swim above the rain.
Out of work and no unemployment.
A mother with five kids living in a studio apartment.
Getting over a broken heart,
Being on death row waiting for a pardon.
Growing old, death and dying.
Diagnosed with cancer, mythology of color,
Being raised without a father,
Losing your baby brother.
Mom working two full-time jobs;
Deadbeat dads trying to live large.
Vietnam war, being crazy and insane.
I write about things that are true to life
Not always a happy ending, just real life.

Order Form

Mail/Send Book(s) to: _____

Street Address: _____

City/State/Zip: _____

Please send (___) copy(s) of "Healing Through Poetry" by Deborah La'Sassier @ $15.00 each.

Total Enclosed $_____

* add mailing/shipping charge of $3.50 per book

I would like the book autographed by the author
Yes_____ No_____

Personalize to_____

* allow 2-3 weeks for delivery

Make checks payable to:
Deborah La'Sassier
39 Frost Valley Drive
East Patchogue, NY 11772

email:dreamlady72@yahoo.com